MUSIC BY GERSHWIN

MUSIC BY

GERSHWIN

Notice:

Composers, arrangers, lyricists, editors, and publishers are entitled to fair payment for their work, and it is both unfair and illegal to threaten their livelihoods by unauthorized copying. We kindly request your cooperation.

Acknowledgments:

Our thanks to Arnold Rosen of Warner Bros. Publications whose unfailing patience and encouragement made this book possible.

Editor-in-Chief:	George W. Cooke
Assistant Editor:	Ruth Kaplan
Research:	Katharine H. Glynn and Ruth Kaplan
Music Proofreaders:	Paul Sheftel and Bonnie Laub
Text Proofreader:	Catherine Shute
Art Director:	James A. Harrington
Cover Art:	Adrian Rappin
Music Engravers:	Music Art Co.
Printer:	Kingsport Press
Executive Editor:	T. Douglas Beasley
Music Director:	Felix Greissle

International Standard Book Number: 0-87824-125-6

Library of Congress Number: 75-39382

Manufactured in the United States of America

Foreword

New York City was (and still is) a wonderful place in which to be born and raised. In the early years of this century, as now, there was music in the air. Daily concerts by the world's greatest pianists, singers, and orchestras have long been accepted as a matter of course by New Yorkers. It is no wonder that George Gershwin's unusual musical gifts flourished in this stimulating city environment into which he was born on September 26, 1898.

As a boy, Gershwin listened to music wherever he heard it, in Carnegie Hall, Cooper Union, City College, the Waldorf Astoria, Brooklyn Academy of Music, Ziegfeld Follies, Harlem clubs, Coney Island band concerts. He heard gypsy violinists at Roumanian restaurants, attended Yiddish musicals, Jewish weddings, Broadway musical extravaganzas, and summer concerts in Catskill Mountain resorts. He attended performances by Josef Lhevinne, Efrem Zimbalist, Josef Hofmann, and dozens of other outstanding soloists and orchestras.

George seems to have learned to play the piano even before he began lessons with Miss Green at the age of 12. He advanced quickly to become a pupil of the great piano teacher Charles Hambitzer, who recognized that George was a musical genius and taught him without fee. Hambitzer trained George in the classics and urged him to become a concert pianist. Hambitzer also sent George to another distinguished piano teacher Edward Kilenyi, to study music theory. Gershwin's piano teachers recognized the boy's great musical gifts and noted his burning interest in ragtime and jazz, but they encouraged him to study the classics. Kilenyi explained to the boy that a solid classical training would enable him to experiment freely and create popular music with insight and intelligence. With the encouragement of his piano teachers, George kept a scrapbook of great concert artists whose concerts he attended.

Although he dropped out of the High School of Commerce when he was only 15, George did not stop growing intellectually. Long evenings of animated discussion of ideas were his in the company of cultivated friends in Greenwich Village and elsewhere. Through his apprenticeship as a song plugger for sheet music publishers, and as a rehearsal pianist for Broadway shows, Gershwin also met scores of famous musicians, writers, actors, singers, and artists of all types of temperament, training, and background, and all degrees of talent. It was with his brilliant friend Irving Caesar that he created his first big song sensation, *Swanee,* which was popularized everywhere by the performances and recordings of another friend, Al Jolson.

George was paid for practicing eight hours a day and more, as it were, in his first job as a player of sheet music for prospective customers, when he was hired by the music publisher Remick. At the same time, he was already writing his own music and by the time he was 18 he was able to quit work as a song plugger in order to compose and study music full time. Still, he played at parties, hotels, rehearsals for musical comedies, wherever a pianist was needed, and in the process his unique keyboard style began to be noted by Victor Herbert, Sigmund Romberg, Jerome Kern, Irving Berlin, and many others. Soon he was collaborating with them on Broadway musical revues. It was not long before Gershwin was composing smash musical comedies of his own. The world will long remember the catchy tunes he composed for his Broadway shows such as *Lady Be Good!, Funny Face,* and *Girl Crazy.*

In addition to musical comedies, Gershwin hoped to write operatic music, and selected as his material Black and Jewish themes from the two ethnic heritages to which he felt closest. His first effort, *Blue Monday,* was an unsuccessful opera based on Black motifs. It foreshadowed *Porgy and Bess,* which was not an instant success, but was eventually to become our most popular American opera, and to enjoy performances all over the world. Gershwin signed a contract with the Metropolitan Opera to create *The Dybbuk,* an opera based on a Jewish folk story, but the work was never completed because the literary rights were assigned to an Italian composer. Critics have noted that the Black and Jewish musical strains seemed to have merged in Gershwin's music, just as the music of the two cultures merged in his day-to-day listening experiences in New York.

George Gershwin's Broadway musicals and operas were to be supplemented by a major piano concerto, the *Rhapsody in Blue,* followed by the *Concerto in F,* and the symphonic tone poem, *An American in Paris.* It was the *Rhapsody in Blue,* first performed in 1925 that brought Gershwin to the high point of his popular acclaim. Other concert works were his *Second Rhapsody, Preludes for Piano,* and *Cuban Overture.*

Despite his great popular and financial success, Gershwin felt a continuing sense of musical inadequacy and so he studied with composers Joseph Schillinger and Rubin Goldmark as well as with Professor Ernest Hutchenson of what is now the Juilliard School. It was typical of Gershwin that he could be working on musical comedy numbers with Oscar Hammerstein II and others, while at the same time he was composing serious concert works. He saw no unbridgeable chasm between popular and serious music.

Many of Gershwin's melodies have long outlived the inferior musical plays and revues in which they were originally set. He broke away from run-of-the-mill comedies with his social satire *Strike Up the Band,* a remarkable work in the tradition of Gilbert and Sullivan, but quite new and original on the American musical comedy stage. Based on a play by George S. Kaufman, *Strike Up the Band* is a forceful attack on government corruption, a satire on senseless wars and the pro-war mentality, and as such it has gained even more relevance in our own time. This original musical form was another first in a long line of important musical creations from the vital imagination of George Gershwin, with amusing lyrics by his brother Ira, lyrics so witty that they have been published separately as a book of poems.

Strike Up the Band, Of Thee I Sing, and *Let 'Em Eat Cake,* are Gershwin's three social satires. They ridicule stupid politicians, the empty slogans of ineffective political parties, and international conflicts fomented by vested economic interests. They seemed particularly to the point during the early years of the Great Depression when government seemed paralyzed. *Of Thee I Sing,* Gershwin's most successful musical, was revived on Broadway in 1952, off-Broadway in 1962, and was presented on television in 1972.

Gershwin was first and foremost a composer, but he enjoyed the limelight as a performer and conductor on occasion. As a performer he was tireless. He tended to dominate parties and social groups with his ability to improvise endlessly on the piano with an extraordinary skill that won the admiration of many other composers.

As a concert pianist, he performed before enormous audiences with great success. The public loved him. He began his important public performances by accompanying the Canadian opera singer Eva Gauthier at an historic concert in Aeolian Hall in New York in 1923. Art songs by Bartok, Hindemith, Schoenberg, and others appeared on the same program with popular American songs by Irving Berlin and, of course, by George Gershwin, the point being to demonstrate that American popular songs could be compared favorably to the works of the leading European composers.

The next year Gershwin played his *Rhapsody in Blue* with the Paul Whiteman orchestra, also in Aeolian Hall, to tremendous public acclaim. In 1927, Gershwin began to offer concerts of his own music at Lewisohn Stadium on the City College campus in Manhattan. Crowds at these concerts numbered as many as 17,000, with thousands turned away. In 1934, he went on tour, performing in Boston, Toronto, Cleveland, Detroit, Chicago, Milwaukee, Omaha, Kansas City, St. Louis, Louisville, Cincinatti, Pittsburgh, Washington, and other cities. Later, he also played in San Francisco,

Seattle, Berkeley, and Los Angeles.

Gershwin's career as a recording artist started as a teenager, when he traveled to New Jersey on Saturdays to cut rolls for player pianos. A number of his piano-roll transcriptions still exist, as well as several recordings of *Rhapsody in Blue.*

As a conductor, Gershwin confined himself to directing orchestral performances of his own compositions. His performance and conducting skills were inadequate for concert performances except in the case of his own compositions, where he excelled, but his ability to sight-read seems to have been limited, and his musical education was just too scrappy to qualify him as a concert pianist or conductor *per se.* He enjoyed conducting opening-night performances of his musicals and he conducted the New York Philharmonic Orchestra at a Gershwin concert, and did a benefit at the New York Metropolitan Opera House, as well as conducting other symphony orchestras.

Suddenly, in 1937, at the age of 38, George Gershwin was dead of a brain tumor.

It seems likely that Gershwin, had he lived, would have contributed a large number of new and original works to the world, concertos, operas, musicals, perennial hit tunes. We can be thankful for the scope of his genius and for the large body of material he left as his heritage. A few unpublished works still remain to be placed before the public. We have included in this volume two of his more recently published posthumous works, the *Impromptu in Two Keys,* and *Two Waltzes in C.*

We believe George Gershwin's work and the example he set by his dedication to the piano and to music will continue to inspire a new generation of pianists and performers. We hope this book will also bring much pleasure and fond memories to those who lived during his lifetime.

Chronology

September 26, 1898	Jacob Gershovitz, better known as George Gershwin, is born to Russian-Jewish immigrants, Morris Gershovitz and Rose Bruskin, in Brooklyn, New York. A first child, Ira, had been born to the Gershovitz couple on December 6, 1896. Then came Arthur on March 14, 1900, and their sister, Frances, September 26, 1908.
1910	The Gershovitz (then Gershvin, later to become Gershwin) family now lives on Second Avenue, New York City. They constantly move from place to place and father Morris is in and out of businesses so often that even the family finds it difficult to keep track of his enterprises. The Gershwins decide to buy a second-hand upright piano on the installment plan so that the older and more serious brother, Ira, can take lessons. George, however, shows an immediate love and natural ability for the piano and he, too, begins to take lessons at 12 years of age from a Miss Green, the neighborhood piano teacher, and then with a Mr. Goldfarb.
1913	George is introduced by a friend to well-known piano teacher Charles Hambitzer who begins to cultivate the boy's talents and directs him in the area of classical music. Later on he also studies theory with Edward Kilenyi, Sr. Even after many years of fame and recognition, George continues to seek instruction in piano theory and technique.
1914	George drops out of the High School of Commerce where, to please his mother, he has been studying bookkeeping, typewriting, and shorthand, and moves over to that famous sheet-music publishing street, Tin Pan Alley, where he is hired, at age 15, as a song "plugger" for music publisher Jerome H. Remick and Company. George earns $15 per week and supplements his income by making player piano rolls in New Jersey.
1916	The youthful song plugger becomes a "pop" composer with his first published ditty, *When You Want 'Em, You Can't Get 'Em; When You've Got 'Em, You Don't Want 'Em.* Harry von Tilzer Music Publishing Company pays George the grand total of $5 in royalties.
1918	George gets his first big job as a composer when he's hired by T.B. Harms Company at $35 per week. Before this, he gets a real

taste of the theater by touring as an accompanist with vaudeville star Louise Dresser. He also takes on jobs as a theater rehearsal pianist where he meets many distinguished composers, some of whom recognize the great talent of the youth. During a six-week tour of the musical *Ladies First* with Nora Bayes (George as her accompanist), the first George-Ira collaboration, *The Real American Folk Song [Is a Rag]* gains attention but is dropped early in the show's New York run. The song does not gain attention for another 40 years until it is published in 1959.

1919   Producer Alex A. Aarons commissions George to write a musical comedy score for *La La Lucille;* the hit song is *Nobody But You.* For the October opening of the new Capitol Theatre in New York City, George writes *Swanee* but nothing happens to this song until top showman Al Jolson introduces it in *Sinbad* at the Winter Garden. In less than one year, the money brought in from sheet music and recording sales of *Swanee* earns thousands of dollars for George.

1920-1924   Producer George White, firmly convinced of Gershwin's talent engages him to write the music for the *George White Scandals,* one of the popular musical revues of the era. During this period, George composes music for part or all of some two dozen Broadway musicals. *Lady Be Good!,* late in 1924, is his best-known musical from this five-year period.

February 12, 1924   The world of music is forever electrified with the introduction of Gershwin's *Rhapsody in Blue* at an all-American jazz concert presented by Paul Whiteman in Aeolian Hall as "An Experiment in Modern Music." The *Rhapsody* had been composed by Gershwin and orchestrated by Ferde Grofé just weeks before the actual first performance.

1925   Gershwin appears as piano soloist at Carnegie Hall to perform his new *Concerto in F,* with Walter Damrosch conducting the New York Symphony Orchestra.

1926-1927   The Gershwin brothers are involved in several musical productions including *Oh, Kay!,* the first version of *Strike Up the Band* and *Funny Face.* On December 4, 1926, Gershwin presents five *Preludes* at a Hotel Roosevelt recital with contralto Mme. Marguerite d'Alvarez. Three of the *Preludes* are later published (1927) as *Preludes for Piano.*

December 13, 1928   After a very successful show *Rosalie,* and a not so very successful show *Treasure Girl,* Gershwin performs with the New York

Philharmonic at Carnegie Hall, his tone poem *An American in Paris* under the baton of Walter Damrosch.

1930   The notable second version of *Strike Up the Band* opens on January 14. *Girl Crazy* opens in October to excellent notices. The brothers journey to Hollywood in November in a plush, private railroad car, to write music and words for the movie musical *Delicious,* starring Janet Gaynor and Charles Farrell.

1931   *Of Thee I Sing* opens on December 26 at the Music Box Theater. It introduces a new form of musical comedy to the stage. In the spring of the following year, *Of Thee I Sing* is awarded the Pulitzer Prize for drama and the $1,000 prize money is divided among the authors of the book, George S. Kaufman, Morrie Ryskind, and lyricist Ira Gershwin. The committee decides that the music should not be included in the judging, and so George Gershwin's contribution to this great production is not officially recognized.

1932   Gershwin composes two more serious pieces. His *Second Rhapsody* for orchestra and piano is first performed by the Boston Symphony on January 29, Serge Koussevitzky conducting and George Gershwin at the piano. Gershwin's second new work, the *Cuban Overture* is first performed on August 16 at Lewisohn Stadium in New York with Albert Coates conducting the New York Philharmonic.

October 10, 1935   A crowning achievement in music—Gershwin's American opera *Porgy and Bess* is produced by the Theatre Guild. The libretto is by DuBose Heyward with lyrics by Heyward and Ira Gershwin.

1936   The Gershwins are lured back to Hollywood, where they are surrounded by some of the most famous people in the creative arts. They do two more movies, *Shall We Dance* and *A Damsel in Distress,* and then begin work on the Samuel Goldwyn production of *The Goldwyn Follies.*

July, 1937   George has been complaining of terrible headaches but his doctors find him to be in excellent health. On July 9, he suddenly goes into a coma and doctors at Los Angeles' Cedars of Lebanon Hospital discover a brain tumor. Gershwin dies at the age of 38, about five hours after emergency surgery is performed, on the morning of July 11. Mourners numbering in the thousands attend simultaneous funeral services on the West Coast and in New York City on July 15. They include the greatest names in music, theater, and politics. The Hollywood movie studios pay final tribute with a moment of silence as the twin funeral services begin.

Table of Contents

Popular Songs

Swanee 1

Somebody Loves Me 7

Oh, Lady Be Good! 11

The Man I Love 15

Fascinating Rhythm 21

Maybe 27

Someone to Watch Over Me 31

The Babbitt and The Bromide 37

'S Wonderful 43

Embraceable You 47

Bidin' My Time 53

I Got Rhythm 57

Strike Up the Band 61

I've Got a Crush on You 67

Of Thee I Sing 71

Love Is Sweeping the Country 75

Let's Call the Whole Thing Off 79

Nice Work If You Can Get It 85

A Foggy Day 91

Gershwin Improvisations of Popular Songs

Swanee 99

'S Wonderful 103

Strike Up the Band 107

I Got Rhythm 111

Recital Works

Prelude I 119

Prelude II 123

Prelude III 127

Two Waltzes in C 131

Impromptu in Two Keys 139

Rhapsody in Blue 145

*A Note on the Cover Painting
"Music by Gershwin," by Adrian Rappin*

The painting reproduced on the cover of this book depicts the life of George Gershwin. To the right we have a glimpse of the typical Lower East Side neighborhood in which Gershwin spent his boyhood. We see the old brick tenements with shops on the first floor and walk-up apartments above, iron fire escapes anchored to the facade of the buildings. George was living in such a building when the family's first piano was hoisted up through the second-floor window.

In the distance we see a romanticized version of the famous Manhattan skyline, a symbol of opportunity and success for artists, writers, and composers, always visible from the Lower East Side.

To the left in the background, we view a corner of Tin Pan Alley, [28th Street in Manhattan] where Gershwin began his career at the age of 15, playing the piano for prospective customers of sheet music.

The musical represented on the stage in the center of the painting is one of Gershwin's great Broadway shows Strike Up the Band.

In the foreground we see Gershwin conducting a symphony orchestra with the piano awaiting his solo performance. The painter has brilliantly illustrated Gershwin's career, from humble beginnings to Tin Pan Alley, from Tin Pan Alley to the Broadway stage, and finally, to the concert hall, the culmination of Gershwin's dream to create serious American music inspired by jazz.

Adrian Rappin, the artist, was born in New York City in 1934, and studied in Europe at the Academy of Fine Arts in Rome, and with Moses Soyer in New York. He received his B.A. from Brandeis University, and also studied at the Art Academy of Cincinnati, and the Art Student's League. He has been elected to membership in The 50 American Artists, Allied Artists of America, American Artists Professional League, and other distinguished associations.

Rappin's paintings for books published by The University Society, Inc. have won numerous awards, including the 1974 Best of Category Award from the Printing Industries of America. Reproductions of his paintings were used in the New York Times "Christmas Fund for the Neediest" annual campaigns in 1967, 1968, 1969, and 1970.

His paintings have been exhibited at one-man shows at the Barzansky Gallery and at the Pacem in Terris Gallery in New York City and at various benefit and competitve group exhibits in New York. He has also had shows at the Four Winds Gallery, Kalamazoo, Michigan, and at the Capricorn Galleries, Bethesda, Maryland.

Rappin's works are represented in the permanent collections of Stratford College, Stratford, Virginia; Randolph Macon College, Lynchburg, Virginia; at Lincoln University Art Collection, Oxford, Pennsylvania; Brandeis University Art Collection, Waltham, Massachusetts, Gibbes Gallery, Charleston Museum, Charleston, South Carolina; Staten Island Museum, Staten Island, New York; and at the Kellogg Foundation, Battle Creek, Michigan. Adrian Rappin lives and works in New York City.

Swanee was George Gershwin's first big song hit, written in 1919. It was first sung in a musical show at the Capitol Theater in New York, but not until Gershwin's friend Al Jolson heard this song and incorporated it into one of his shows, *Sinbad,* did the tune become a national favorite.

The recording sold two million records and the publisher sold a million copies of the sheet music. Lyrics are by Irving Caesar with whom Gershwin frequently collaborated in his early days as a composer. Gershwin had written many songs before *Swanee,* and had even composed a musical, but this song made him famous.

SWANEE

Words by
IRVING CAESAR

Music by
GEORGE GERSHWIN

4

George Gershwin and Irving Berlin. Gershwin and Berlin were good friends. *Culver Pictures.*

Somebody Loves Me was the hit tune of *George White's Scandals of 1924,* an annual Broadway musical revue. Gershwin wrote a dozen songs for this show, one of the most lavishly staged and produced extravaganzas of its time, and a competitor of the famous *Ziegfeld Follies.*

Rhapsody in Blue had just been given its sensational first performance in February of 1924. It was characteristic of Gershwin to be able to write popular tunes at the same time he was composing piano concertos.

SOMEBODY LOVES ME

Words by
B.G. DeSYLVA
and BALLARD MacDONALD

Music by
GEORGE GERSHWIN

When this world be-gan It was Heav-en's plan,

There should be a girl for ev-'ry sin-gle man;

8

Lady, Be Good! was the title of a very successful musical in 1924, in which, for the first time, George and his brother Ira created the complete music and lyrics for a show. This marked the beginning of an enduring partnership. George's musical genius combined with Ira's clever lyrics resulted in many smash hits on Broadway, and the dozens of favorite songs that we cherish today, long after the Broadway productions for which they were written have been forgotten.

Oh, Lady Be Good!

Words by
IRA GERSHWIN

Music by
GEORGE GERSHWIN

I'm all a - lone in this big cit - y
So let's put two and two to - geth - er

I tell you I'm just a lone - some babe in the wood
I tell you I'm just a lone - some babe in the wood

So la - dy be good _____ to me! _____
So la - dy be good _____ to

me! _____

14

The Man I Love, now a popular standard familiar to millions, was not successful at first. It failed as a show tune in *Lady, Be Good!* and in *Strike Up the Band.* Only after Lady Mountbatten heard the song and asked George Gershwin for a copy to take back with her to England did the song become a hit. It was soon the rage of London. After enjoying great success in London and Paris, singer Helen Morgan popularized the song in New York, and soon it swept the nation.

THE MAN I LOVE

Words by
IRA GERSHWIN

Music by
GEORGE GERSHWIN

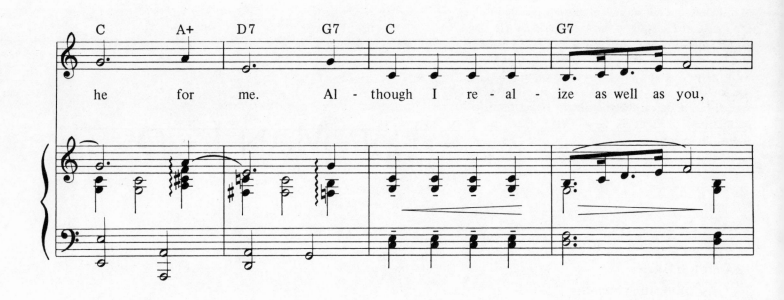

he for me. Al - though I re - al - ize as well as you,

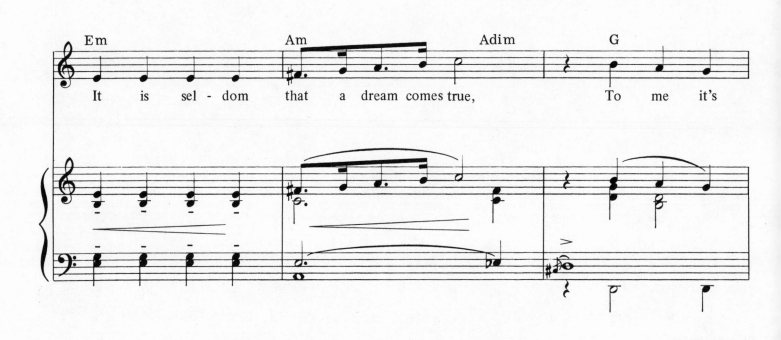

It is sel - dom that a dream comes true, To me it's

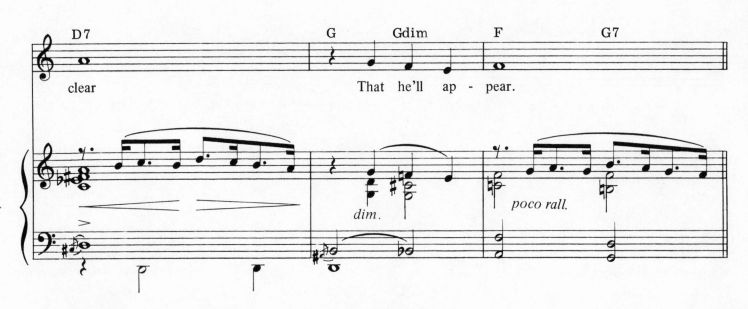

clear That he'll ap - pear.

dim. *poco rall.*

16

And though it seems ab-surd, I know we both won't say a

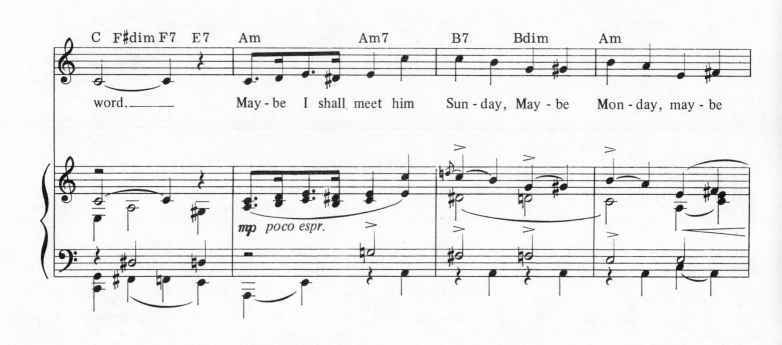

word.___ May - be I shall meet him Sun - day, May - be Mon - day, may - be

not; Still I'm sure to meet him one day, May - be Tues - day will be

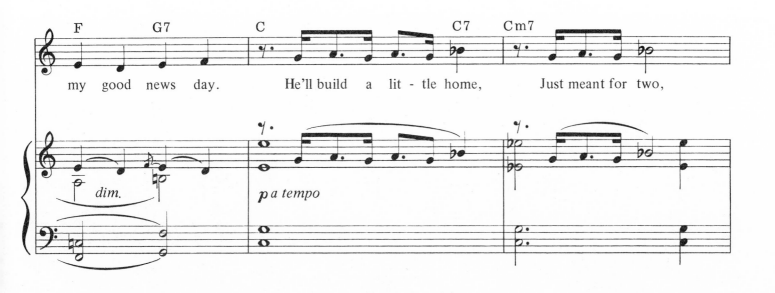

my good news day. He'll build a lit - tle home, Just meant for two,

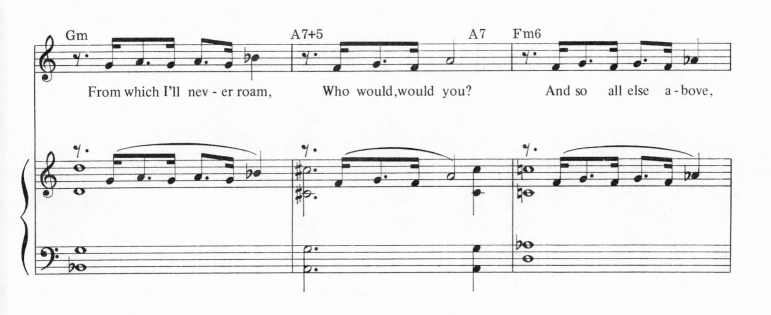

From which I'll nev - er roam, Who would, would you? And so all else a - bove,

I'm wait - ing for the man I love. love._____

19

The shifting meters in this song from *Lady, Be Good!* are indeed fascinating. Fascinating, too, was the young song-and-dance team featured in the show—Fred Astaire and his sister Adele. Producers of *Lady, Be Good!* were Alex Aarons and Vincent Freedley, who worked on many Gershwin shows. *Lady, Be Good!* was a solid success in New York, where it opened at the Liberty Theater on December 1, 1924. Later it was taken to London for a very enthusiastic reception by English audiences. The movie version appeared in 1945.

FASCINATING RHYTHM

Words by
IRA GERSHWIN

Music by
GEORGE GERSHWIN

When it - 'll drive me in - sane.   Comes in the morn - ing With -

out an - y warn - ing,   And hangs a - round all   day.

I'll have   to sneak   up to   it,   Some-day   and speak   up to   it,

I hope   it lis - tens when   I   say:

"Fas-ci-nat-ing Rhy-thm You've got me on the go! Fas-ci-

nat-ing Rhy-thm I'm all a-qui-ver. What a mess you're mak-ing! The

neigh-bors want to know why I'm al-ways shak-ing Just like a fli-ver.

Each morn-ing I get up__ with the sun, (Start a hop-ping nev-er stop-ping)

snap - py!   Oh, how I long to be ____ the man
I used to be!   Fas - ci - nat - ing Rhy - thm,   Oh,
won't you stop pick - ing on me?"
me?"

Rehearsing for *Rosalie*

Left to right: Jack Donahue, George Gershwin, Sigmund Romberg, Marilyn Miller, and Flo Ziegfeld.

Rosalie (1928) was an extremely successful Broadway musical for which George Gershwin composed the music, with some songs contributed by Sigmund Romberg, the great Hungarian-born composer of operettas. Lyrics were by P.G. Wodehouse and Ira Gershwin. Marilyn Miller starred in the show with Jack Donahue. *Rosalie* was produced by Flo Ziegfeld, originator of the famous *Ziegfeld Follies,* an elaborately staged musical revue starting in 1907, which ran for more than 20 years on Broadway.   *Culver Pictures.*

When the famous English actress Gertrude Lawrence heard that her friend George Gershwin was writing the music for a new Broadway show to be called *Oh, Kay!*, she immediately accepted the offer from producers Aaron and Freedley to play the lead. Gertrude Lawrence was to become one of America's great leading ladies for some 30 years, until her death while starring in *The King and I* in the 1950's.

MAYBE

Words by
IRA GERSHWIN

Music by
GEORGE GERSHWIN

Someone to Watch Over Me was one of the highlights of an outstanding musical score Gershwin wrote for *Oh, Kay!* The show opened at the Imperial Theater in New York on November 8, 1926. The book was by Guy Bolten and P.G. Wodehouse. Noted critic Brooks Atkinson described the show as "a marvel of its kind." Lyrics were by Ira Gershwin and Howard Dietz. The show was taken to London where George heard its closing performance in 1928, while on a trip to compose a new work, *An American in Paris*, his famous symphonic tone poem.

SOMEONE TO WATCH OVER ME

Words by
IRA GERSHWIN

Music by
GEORGE GERSHWIN

had in mind. Look - ing ev - 'ry - where, Have - n't

found him yet; He's the big af - fair I can - not for - get.

On - ly man I ev - er Think of with re - gret.

I'd like to add his in - i - tial to my

The Babbitt and the Bromide is a biting satire on shallow and selfish people who only pretend to be interested in the welfare of others. It was sung in alternating phrases by Adele and Fred Astaire in Gershwin's highly successful musical *Funny Face* in 1927. The "Babbitt" alludes to an insensitive and grasping businessman, George F. Babbitt, the main character in the famous novel *Babbitt* by Sinclair Lewis, published in 1922. A "Bromide" is a person who substitutes empty phrases and meaningless small talk for sincere feeling.

THE BABBIT AND THE BROMIDE

From "Funny Face"

Words by
IRA GERSHWIN

Music by
GEORGE GERSHWIN

They / That / A
both were sol - id   cit - i - zens they
they had both de - vel - oped in ten
harp each one was   car - ry - ing and

both had been a - round,   And / as they spoke you clear - ly saw their
years, there was no   doubt,   And / so, of course, they had an aw - ful
both were wear - ing   wings,   And / this is what they said as they were

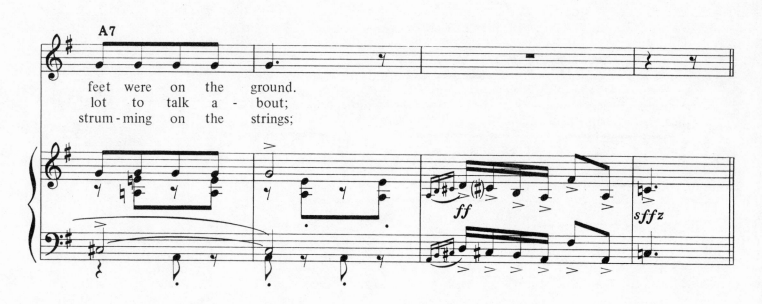

feet were   on the   ground.
lot to   talk a - bout;
strum - ming on the   strings;

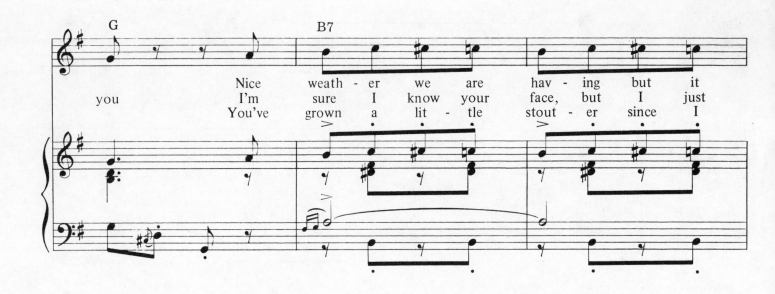

Nice weath - er we are hav - ing but it
You've sure grown a lit - tle stout - er since I
I'm know your face, but I just

gives me such a pain; I've tak - en my um -
can't re - call your name, Well, how've you been old
saw you last, I think; You must come o - ver

brel - la, so, of course, it does - n't rain. Heigh - ho! That's
boy? You're look - ing just a - bout the same.
some - day and we'll have a lit - tle drink.

George Gershwin rehearses with the Los Angeles Philharmonic Orchestra. Gershwin was the piano soloist with the orchestra in two all-Gershwin programs in 1936. *Culver Pictures*.

'S Wonderful was the hit tune of the 1927 musical *Funny Face,* which ran on Broadway for 244 performances and then went on to London. Maurice Ravel, the great French composer attended *Funny Face* in New York and then asked to meet George Gershwin. Gershwin played the piano for hours for Ravel and expressed a wish to study with the French composer. Ravel greatly admired Gershwin's talent and keyboard skills and indicated that Gershwin did not need any lessons from him. After completing *Funny Face,* George went to Europe, where he met many leading composers such as Igor Stravinsky, Sergei Prokofiev, Alexandre Tansman, Darius Milhaud, and Francis Poulenc, all of whom recognized Gershwin's genius.

'S WONDERFUL

Words by
IRA GERSHWIN

Music by
GEORGE GERSHWIN

Girl Crazy opened at the Alvin Theater in New York on October 14, 1930. The show, starring Ginger Rogers and Ethel Merman, was an instant success. Some of the relatively unknown young musicians in the orchestra, whose names later became household words, were Glenn Miller, Jimmy Dorsey, and Benny Goodman.

Gershwin had a contract with the Metropolitan Opera to write an opera entitled *The Dybbuk,* but when the literary rights to the story were assigned to an Italian composer, Gershwin wrote *Girl Crazy* instead. He then moved to Beverly Hills to compose for the movies.

EMBRACEABLE YOU

Words by
IRA GERSHWIN

Music by
GEORGE GERSHWIN

Don't be a naugh-ty ba-by, Come to pa-pa, Come to pa-pa, do!

My sweet em-brace-a-ble

you!

you!

On the movie set for *Shall We Dance*
Seated are Fred Astaire, Ginger Rogers, and George Gershwin.
Standing left to right are Hermes Pan (Dance Director), Mark Sandrick (Film Director), Ira Gershwin, and Nathaniel Shilkret (Musical Director). The movie *Shall We Dance* was released in 1937. *Culver Pictures.*

Bidin My Time was sung by a quartet known as *The Foursome* in the musical *Girl Crazy* produced on Broadway in 1930. *Girl Crazy* ran for 272 performances despite its ridiculous plot, and the hit tunes of the show have remained popular to this day. Millions of Americans saw the three movie versions of *Girl Crazy,* which brought Gershwin's music to Americans across the nation. The first Hollywood movie was released in 1932; the second, starring Judy Garland, Mickey Rooney, and June Allyson was distributed to theaters in 1936; and *When the Boys Meet the Girls,* the 1965 version of *Girl Crazy* featured Connie Francis, Liberace, and Louis Armstrong in leading roles.

BIDIN' MY TIME

Words by
IRA GERSHWIN

Music by
GEORGE GERSHWIN

54

Ethel Merman made her memorable debut in *Girl Crazy* by singing *I Got Rhythm*. One of a genre of lighthearted songs asserting the superiority of music, nature, and love over material wealth and power, *I Got Rhythm* has been a popular favorite with singers and audiences for the past 50 years. The musical in which this song first appeared was a satire on the rough-and-ready western frontier of an earlier America.

I GOT RHYTHM

Words by
IRA GERSHWIN

Music by
GEORGE GERSHWIN

The musical satire *Strike Up the Band* was written in 1926 and opened in 1927 to short runs in Long Branch, New Jersey, and Philadelphia, but enjoyed little success until its revision for Broadway in 1930. A biting satire on war and corruption in business and government, the show was toned down for the 1930 audiences. At any rate, criticism of the social system was greeted with more respect during the years of the Great Depression than it had been in the prosperous years of the Roaring Twenties.

STRIKE UP THE BAND

Words by
IRA GERSHWIN

Music by
GEORGE GERSHWIN

Rum - ta - ta - tum - tum, Rum - ta - ta - tum - tum - tum! _____

Very marked

Refrain:

Let the drums roll out! _____ Let the trum - pet call! _____

(Boom, boom, boom!) (Ta - ta -

While the peo - ple shout! _____ Strike up the

ra - ta - ta - ta!) (Hoo - ray!)

band! _____ Hear the cym - bals ring! _____

(Imitation of Trpt.)

(spoken)

(Shouted)

I've Got A Crush on You was actually written in 1928 for *Treasure Girl,* a show with a silly plot that had only a short run on Broadway. The next year Gershwin salvaged this tune, as was his custom when he wrote a song too good to die with a bad play, and with writer Morrie Ryskind skillfully incorporated *I've Got A Crush on You* into the second version of *Strike Up the Band,* which enjoyed a successful run at the Times Square Theater in New York.

I'VE GOT A CRUSH ON YOU

Words by
IRA GERSHWIN

Music by
GEORGE GERSHWIN

Could you care ___ for a cun-ning cot-tage we could share? ___ The world will par - don my mush, 'cause I've got a crush, my ba - by, on you. ___ I've got a you.

Of Thee I Sing was greeted by the critics as a work of art quite new and original in American theater. The plot, characters, social theme and music were so skillfully joined into a coherent whole that its literary co-authors George S. Kaufman, Morrie Ryskind, and Ira Gershwin won the Pulitzer Prize in Letters for 1932, taking the laurels away from Eugene O'Neil's *Mourning Becomes Electra*, which also made its stage debut in that year. Even though George Gershwin did not receive a prize as composer of the musical score, a reexamination of the play today will quickly convince the reader that it was the music and not the literary work which made the musical so stimulating to audiences and critics.

OF THEE I SING

Words by
IRA GERSHWIN

Music by
GEORGE GERSHWIN

Love Is Sweeping the Country was one of the hit tunes in *Of Thee I Sing*. The show opened on December 26, 1931, at the Music Box Theater in New York City, after tryouts in Boston, where it was a sensation. Three months later the Pulitzer Prize Committee selected it as "the original American play performed in New York which shall best represent the educational value and power of the stage." In the show, John P. Wintergreen runs for President on a platform of love in a spoof of American politics and campaign strategies by political parties. New York Mayor Jimmy Walker attended the opening night, as did Governor Al Smith and other politicians.

LOVE IS SWEEPING THE COUNTRY

Words by
IRA GERSHWIN

Music by
GEORGE GERSHWIN

Refrain:

Love is sweep - ing the coun - try, _____ Waves are hug -
ging the shore, _____ All the sex - es From Maine to Tex -
_____ as Have nev - er known such love be - fore.
See them bill - ing and coo - ing, _____ Like the bird -

This song, considered by many to be one of Gershwin's best, was written for the 1937 movie *Shall We Dance*. Fred Astaire and Ginger Rogers were the stars of the film. The Gershwins moved to Beverly Hills in August 1936 to work on movies. It was George's idea to make enough money on films so that he would no longer have any money worries and he could then devote his full attention to composing major piano works, symphonies, chamber music, and operas. Since boyhood, Gershwin had felt an ardent desire to help create great American concert music, music as good as anything composed in Europe.

LET'S CALL THE WHOLE THING OFF

Words by
IRA GERSHWIN

Music by
GEORGE GERSHWIN

Things have come to a pret-ty pass,— Our ro-mance is grow-ing flat, For you like this and the oth-er— While

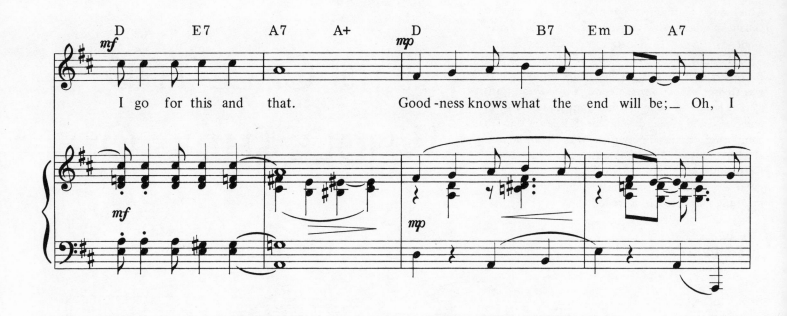

I go for this and that. Good-ness knows what the end will be;— Oh, I

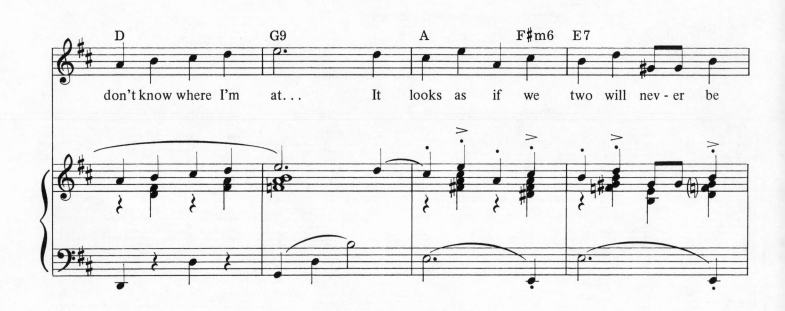

don't know where I'm at... It looks as if we two will nev-er be

one, Some-thing must be done._____

Refrain:

You say ee - ther And I say eye - ther, You say nee - ther And
You say laugh - ter And I say lawf - ter, You say af - ter And

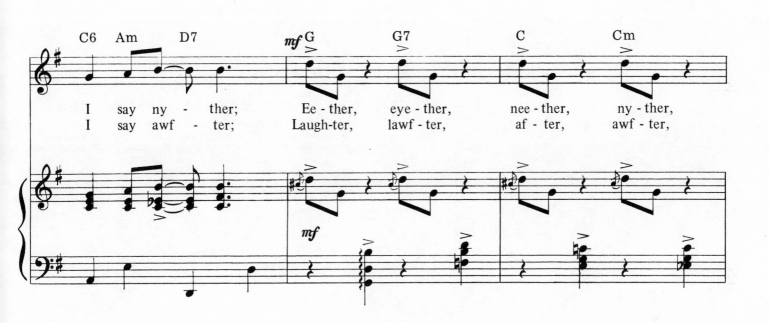

I say ny - ther; Ee - ther, eye - ther, nee - ther, ny - ther,
I say awf - ter; Laugh-ter, lawf - ter, af - ter, awf - ter,

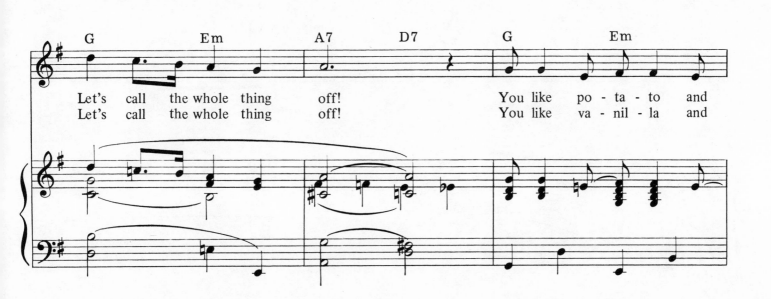

Let's call the whole thing off! You like po - ta - to and
Let's call the whole thing off! You like va - nil - la and

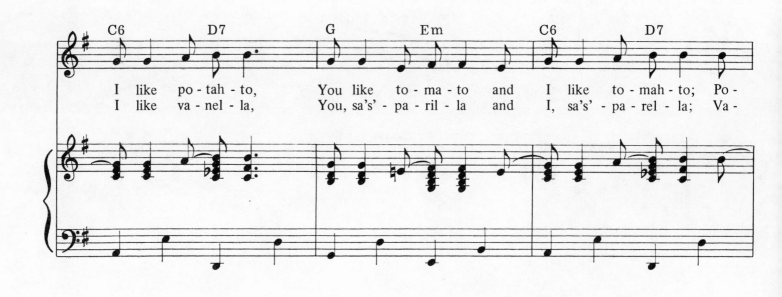

I like po - tah - to,   You like to - ma - to and I like to - mah - to; Po -
I like va - nel - la,   You, sa's' - pa - ril - la and I, sa's' - pa - rel - la; Va -

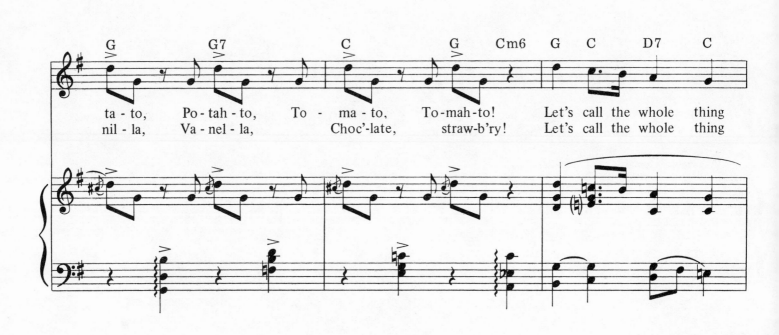

ta - to, Po - tah - to, To - ma - to, To - mah - to! Let's call the whole thing
nil - la, Va - nel - la, Choc'- late, straw - b'ry! Let's call the whole thing

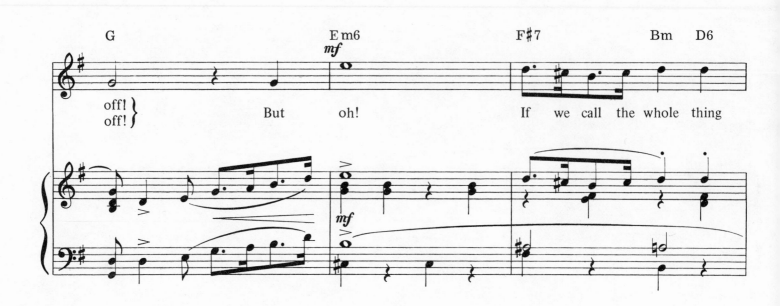

off! }
off! }   But   oh!   If we call the whole thing

off, Then we must part. And oh!

If we ev - er part, Then that might break my heart!

So, if
So, if

you like pa - ja - mas And I like pa - jah - mas,
you go for oys - ters And I go for ers - ters

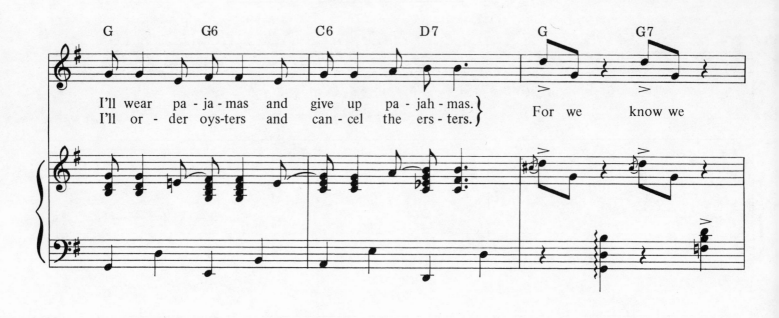

I'll wear pa - ja - mas and give up pa - jah - mas.
I'll or - der oys - ters and can - cel the ers - ters.
For we know we

need each oth - er, So we bet - ter call the call - ing off off.

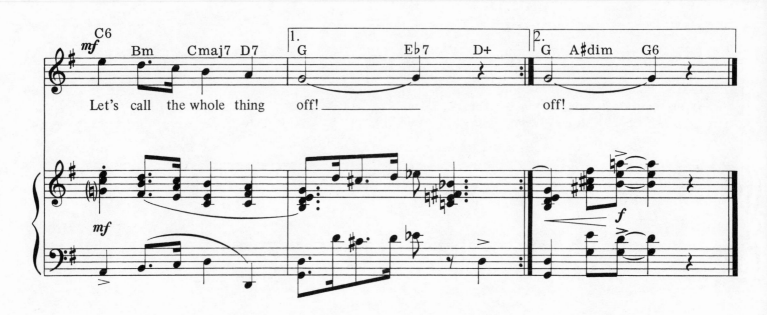

Let's call the whole thing off! _____ off! _____

This song, along with *A Foggy Day,* are the two best remembered songs from Gershwin's score for the 1937 movie *A Damsel in Distress. Nice Work* was sung by Fred Astaire and a female trio. As in the case of the musical shows, Gershwin's tunes have long outlived any interest in the movies themselves.

NICE WORK IF YOU CAN GET IT

Words by
IRA GERSHWIN

Music by
GEORGE GERSHWIN

The man who on - ly lives for mak - ing mon - ey

Lives a life that is - n't nec - es - sar - i - ly sun - ny.

Gershwin works on the score for *Porgy and Bess*, 1935.
Picture courtesy of New York Public Library.

A Foggy Day was composed for the 1937 movie *A Damsel in Distress,* starring Fred Astaire and Joan Fontaine, with gag scenes by George Burns and Gracie Allen. Fred Astaire sang this song in the movie, which was not very successful. Frank Sinatra later took up *A Foggy Day* and has become closely identified with it.

A Foggy Day

Words by
IRA GERSHWIN

Music by
GEORGE GERSHWIN

do? What to do? What to do? The out-look was de-cid-ed-ly blue._____ But as I walked through the fog-gy streets a-lone, It turned out to be the luck-iest day I've known._____

(brighter but warmly)

Refrain:

A fog-gy day_____ in Lon-don town_____

Ira Gershwin wrote lyrics for Kurt Weill, Aaron Copland, Jerome Kern, and other composers, but he is, of course, best known for his collaboration with his brother. *Culver Pictures*.

Improvisations

George Gershwin loved to play the piano and did so on every possible occasion. He frequently entertained at the piano for hours on end at parties and social gatherings for friends and acquaintances. His distinctive style was engaging and inimitable. Most of the leading musicians and composers of his day heard Gershwin play the piano, and they were enthusiastic in their praise of his unusual keyboard skills. He played for Maurice Ravel, Sergei Rachmaninoff, Alexandre Tansman, Jerome Kern, Serge Prokofiev, Victor Herbert, Arturo Toscanini, Serge Koussevitzky, Henry Cowell, Jascha Heifetz, and a long list of others distinguished in the world of music.

Although Gershwin's keyboard improvisations of his own songs were endless, a few of them were written down and published in 1932. Of the 18 published improvisations we have included four here. They clearly indicate the varied and almost limitless possibilities for improvisation with his popular songs.

SWANEE

Music by
GEORGE GERSHWIN
Spirited

Words by
IRVING CAESAR

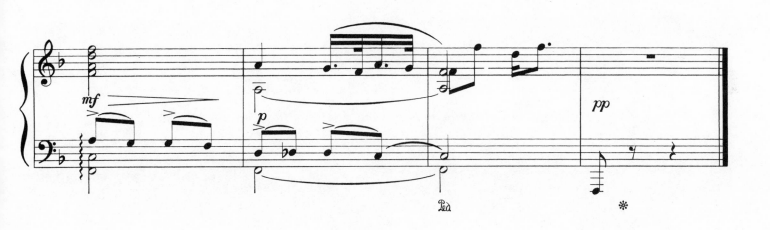

'S Wonderful

Music by
GEORGE GERSHWIN
Liltingly

Words by
IRA GERSHWIN

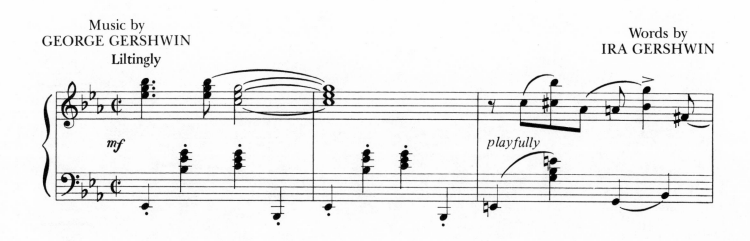

STRIKE UP THE BAND

Words by
IRA GERSHWIN

Music by
GEORGE GERSHWIN

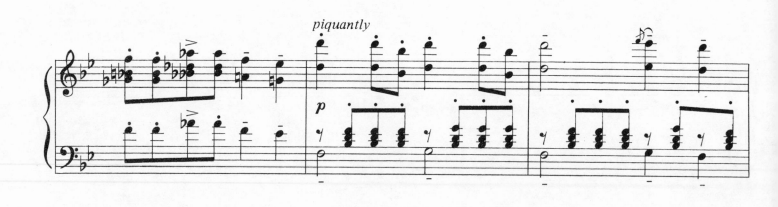

I Got Rhythm

Words by
IRA GERSHWIN

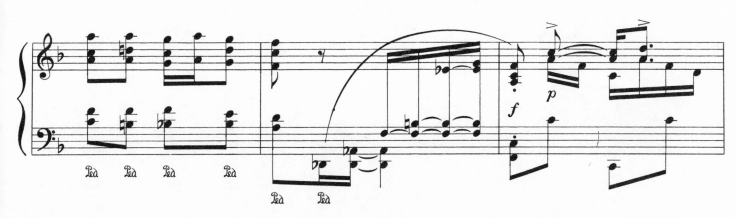

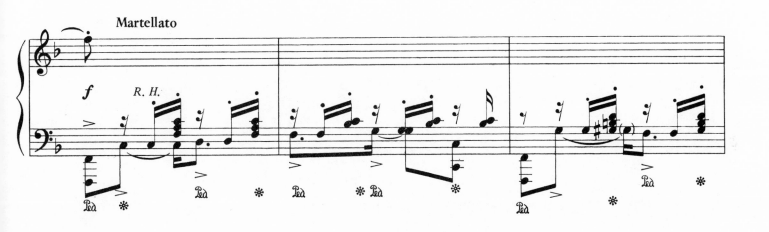

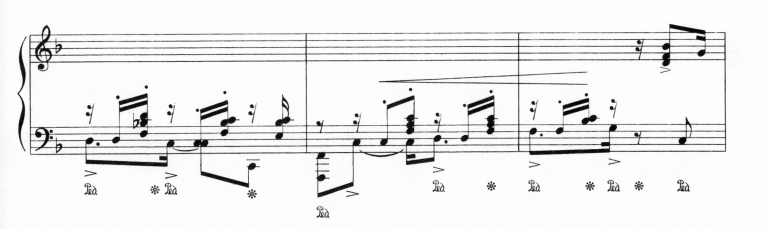

Recital
Works

George Gershwin with the Leo Reisman Orchestra. Gershwin went on tour with the orchestra in 1934, performing in Boston, Toronto, Cleveland, Detroit, Chicago, Milwaukee, Omaha, Kansas City, St. Louis, Louisville, Cincinatti, Pittsburgh, Washington, and elsewhere to great public acclaim. Everyone, it seemed, wanted to hear Gershwin play the piano. *Culver Pictures.*

George Gershwin first presented these *Preludes* to the public in a concert given on December 4, 1926, at the Hotel Roosevelt in New York City. Gershwin shared the concert with singer Marguerite d'Alvarez, and played five of his original preludes. The suite of three preludes as we know it today was published in 1927, and has grown gradually in fame and popularity over the years, until now it is familiar to music lovers around the world. The *Preludes* are often listed in the teaching syllabuses of piano teachers' associations, and have been transcribed for orchestra.

PRELUDE I

By
GEORGE GERSHWIN

PRELUDE II

By
GEORGE GERSHWIN

Andante con moto e poco rubato (M.M. ♩=88)

PIANO

p legato

p

Ped. ✳ Ped. ✳ Ped. ✳ Ped. ✳ *simile*

Optional Version: Reverse Hands

PRELUDE III

By
GEORGE GERSHWIN

Two Waltzes in C was written for a sequence in the musical show *Pardon My English,* but was dropped during the tryouts and was not used or published until 1971.

Pardon My English was hastily thrown together to bring financial relief to George's long-time producers Alex Aarons and Vinton Freedley, but to no avail. The show opened at the Majestic Theater in New York in January of 1933. It ran for only a few weeks and lost money.

TWO WALTZES IN C

Edited by
IRA GERSHWIN

By
GEORGE GERSHWIN

Adapted by
SAUL CHAPLIN

WALTZ I

Moderate

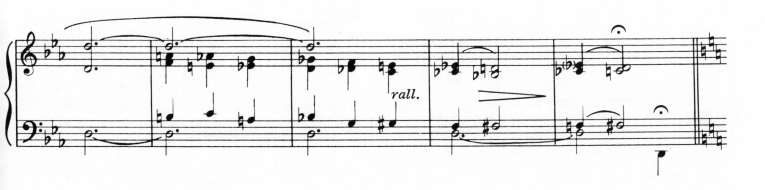

WALTZ II

Moderate

136

Gershwin left behind him a number of unpublished songs and partially completed scores. These manuscripts have been carefully preserved in Beverly Hills by his brother Ira, who has permitted a few of them to be published from time to time. The *Impromptu in Two Keys* is believed to have been composed about 1924 and was intended for use in a later show.

Most of George's holograph (handwritten) scores have been donated to the Library of Congress. Other collections of Gershwin papers may be found at Fisk University, Nashville, Tennessee, and at the University of Texas, Austin. The Museum of the City of New York also has a fine collection of Gershwin memorabilia and sheet music.

IMPROMPTU IN TWO KEYS

By
GEORGE GERSHWIN

Rhapsody in Blue was composed at the piano in 1924, and orchestrated by composer Ferde Grofé for a special concert of American music given by the Paul Whiteman orchestra at Aeolian Hall on 43rd Street in New York City. The Whiteman concert was conceived as a means to promote native American music. The day chosen for the concert was, appropriately enough, Lincoln's birthday. Other composers whose works were performed that day included Victor Herbert, Irving Berlin, and Edward MacDowell. Present at the concert were many famous concert artists and composers, such as Sergei Rachmaninoff, Fritz Kreisler, Leopold Stokowski, Jascha Heifetz, Walter Damrosch, Ernest Bloch, and John Phillip Sousa.

The *Rhapsody* was greeted with a great ovation and has maintained its instant popularity ever since. George Gershwin, the composer of Tin Pan Alley tunes, had made it to the concert hall, and, in the process, had demonstrated to the critics, to other composers, and to the public that jazz and popular music and their composers are worthy of serious study.

The piano solo was revised slightly by Gershwin after the concert to give us the work as we know it today. Several orchestral arrangements have been made, and the *Rhapsody* has been transcribed for various solo instruments, and has been arranged for ballet and dance groups.

The second page of the score of *Rhapsody in Blue* in Gershwin's hand. J.B. stands for Jazz Band.

Rhapsody In Blue

Music by
GEORGE GERSHWIN

PIANO SOLO

145

*) Cut may be made to *) p. 158.

Meno mosso e poco scherzando
(Slower)

157

160

*) Cut may be made to *) p. 165.

Leggiero

Agitato e misterioso

166

Molto stentando

poco a poco rit.

Molto allargando

Bibliography

Hundreds of articles have been written about George Gershwin, and a large number of books devote space to his life and work. This list provides the most basic references for the student and teacher. For a more complete bibliography consult the volume by Charles Schwartz listed below.

1. Armitage, Merle, ed. *George Gershwin*. New York: Longmans, Green, 1938. Tributes to Gershwin by his friends and associates, such as Oscar Hammerstein, II, Arnold Schoenberg, and Paul Whiteman.

2. Ewen, David, *George Gershwin: His Journey to Greatness*. Englewood Cliffs, N.J.: Prentice-Hall, 1970.

3. Ewen, David. *The Story of George Gershwin*. New York: Henry Holt, 1943. A delightful biography of Gershwin for children. Reads like an adventure story.

4. Gershwin, Ira. *Lyrics on Several Occasions*. New York: Alfred A. Knopf, 1959. The text of Ira's many lyrics with interesting recollections by the author of the circumstances under which they were written. Includes lyrics Ira wrote for his brother George and for other composers.

5. Green, Stanley. *The World of Musical Comedy*. Cranbury, New New Jersey: A.S. Barnes and Company, 1968 (revised edition). A history of American musical comedies, major and minor composers, writers, and stage personalities. Devotes one chapter to George and Ira Gershwin.

6. Jablonski, Edward, and Lawrence D. Stewart. *The Gershwin Years*. Garden City, New York: Doubleday & Company, Inc., 1973 (Revised edition). Undoubtedly one of the two best biographies available. Heavily illustrated with rare photographs based on exhaustive research. A pleasure to read.

7. Kimball, Robert, and Alfred Simon. *The Gershwins*. New York: Atheneum, 1973. A splendid, heavily illustrated book about the Gershwins and their friends. Contains dozens of photographs of Gershwin and his associates. Valuable chronological listings of musical productions and individual songs by Gershwin. Not as detailed or as well integrated as the biographies by Schwartz, and by Jablonski and Stewart.

8. Schwartz, Charles. *Gershwin: His Life and Music*. Indianapolis: The Bobbs-Merrill Company, Inc., 1973. A magnificent biography of the composer and a history of his era. Every Gershwin student will want to have a copy of this book. Packed with fascinating and relevant facts about Gershwin and his illustrious circle of friends. Includes an extensive bibliography of journal articles and books relating to Gershwin.

Discography

If you were to ask someone, "What do the following people have in common — Leonard Bernstein, Fats Waller, Liza Minelli, Al Jolson, Jim Nabors, Judy Garland, Arthur Fiedler, Eartha Kitt, Yehudi Menuhin, Guy Lombardo, Count Basie, Andre Kostelanetz, Eddie Fisher, Percy Faith, Billie Holiday, Andre Previn, Benny Goodman, Carroll O'Connor, Paul Whiteman, Barbra Streisand, Glenn Miller, and Frank Sinatra?" The answer would be, "They have all recorded performances of George Gershwin's music."

What they and hundreds of other performers have in common is the legacy of Gershwin's music, which appeals to all kinds of people and all types of performers. This selected list includes recordings of only those works published in this volume. A complete listing of all the recordings of Gershwin's works would run into the thousands. This discography serves as an index of Gershwin's continuing popularity and we hope it will be useful to the student and collector.

Swanee

Bailey, Jim, from the album *Live at Carnegie Hall:* United Artists Records LA146-H2.

Garland, Judy, from the album *Judy at Carnegie Hall:* Capitol Records SWBO-1569. From the album *Judy Garland, Deluxe Set:* Capitol Records STCL-2988. From the album *Judy—Collector's Items:* MCA Records 2-4046. From the album (with Liza Minnelli) *Live at the London Palladium:* Capitol Records ST-11191.

Jolson, Al, from the album *Al Jolson Story Part 2:* MCA Records 2058. From the album *Best of Al Jolson:* MCA Records 2-10002.

Nabors, Jim, from the album *Love Me With All Your Heart:* Columbia Records CS-9358.

Newton, Wayne, from the album *Wayne Newton:* Capitol Records STCL-573.

Somebody Loves Me

Charleston City All Stars, from the album *Roaring 20's—Volume 2:* Westminster Records GAS-68.

Cooper, Bob, from the album *Music of Bob Cooper:* Contemporary Records 7012.

Four Freshmen, from the album *Kenton—Christy—Four Freshmen:* Capitol Records STCL-575.

Garner, Erroll, from the album *Erroll Garner:* Savoy Records 12002.

Heath, Ted, from the album *All Time Top Twelve:* London PS-117.

Hines, Earl, from the album *Fatha and His Flock on Tour:* MPS Records 20749.

Hodges, Johnny, from the album *Johnny Hodges:* Verve Records V6-883.

Light, Enoch, from the album *Roaring Twenties:* ABC Records 746. From the album *Big Band Hits of the 20's:* Project Records QD-5.

Rollini, Adrian, O., from the album *Jazz Holiday:* MCA Records 2-4018.

Shirley, Don, from the album *Don Shirley:* Audio Fidelity 5896.

Smith, Jimmy, from the album *Sounds of Jimmy Smith:* Blue Note Records 81556.

Tatum, Art, from the album *Capitol Jazz Classics—Volume 3:* Capitol M-11028. From the album *Art Tatum—Volume 1:* Crescendo Records 99025. From the album *Art Tatum, Solo Masterpieces:* Pablo Records 265703.

Teagarden, Jack, from the album *Golden Horn of Jack Teagarden:* MCA Records 227.

Oh, Lady Be Good

Basie, Count, from the album *Super Chief:* Columbia Records G-31224. From the album *Best of Count Basie:* MCA Records 2-4050. From the album *For the First Time:* Pablo Records 2310712.

Buck and Bubbles, from the album *Jazz Odyssey:* Columbia Records C3L-33.

Ellis, Herb and Joe Pass, from the album *Two for the Road:* Pablo Records 2310714.

Fitzgerald, Ella, from the album *Ella Sings Gershwin:* MCA Records 215. From the album *Best of Ella:* MCA Records 2-4047.

Fountain, Pete, from the album *Best of Pete Fountain:* MCA Records 2-4032.

Gillespie, Dizzy, from the album *Echoes of an Era—Best of Gershwin:* Roulette Records RE-120. From the album (with J. Carroll) *School Days:* Savoy Records 12204.

Goodman, Benny, Count Basie, and others, from the album *From Spirituals to Swing:* Vanguard Records VSD-47/48.

Goodman, Benny, Septet, from the album *On Stage:* London Records BP-44182/83.

Grierson, Ralph, and Artie Kane, from the album *Gershwin—'S Wonderful:* Angel Records 36083.

Hampton, Lionel, and the All Stars, from the album *Star Dust:* MCA Records 198.

Hawkins, Coleman, from the album *Jazz Pioneers:* Prestige Records 7647.

Heath, Ted, from the album *Swing Is King:* London Records PP-44113.

Menuhin, Y./S., from the album *Jalousie—Music of the 30's:* Angel Records 369968.

Parker, Charlie, from the album *The Charlie Parker Story—Volume 3:* Verve Records 6-8002.

Parker, Charlie, from the album *Return Engagement:* Verve Records V3HB-8840.

Quintette of the Hot Club of France, from the album *Django "1934":* Crescendo Records 9031. From the album *First Recordings:* Prestige Records 7614.

Reinhardt, Django, from the album *Django Reinhardt—Volume 4:* Everest Records 306.

Shaw, Artie, from the album *Best of Artie Shaw:* Victor Records ANLI-1089.

Smith, Jimmy, from the album *New Star, New Sound:* Blue Note Records 81512.

Supersax, from the album *Supersax Plays Bird:* Capitol Records ST-11177.

Wilson, Teddy, from the album *Teddy Wilson and His All Stars:* Columbia Records KG-31617.

The Man I Love

Boston Pops with Arthur Fiedler, from the album *Greatest Hits of the 20's:* Victor Records ARLI-0041. From the album (with Peter Nero) *Greatest Hit Songs:* Victor Records ARLI-0510. From the album *Fiedler and His Friends:* Victor Records LSC-3199.

Burrell, Kenny, from the album *Blue Lights:* Blue Note Records 81597.

Chacksfield, Frank, from the album *The Glory That Was Gershwin:* London Records SP-44194.

Charles, Ray, from the album *Genius After Hours:* Atlantic Recording Corp. 1369.

Cher, from the album *Bittersweet White Light:* MCA Records 2101.

Cole, Nat King, from the album *Capitol Jazz Classics—Volume 8:* Capitol Records M-11033.

Crossan, Jack, from the album *Keyboard Kaleidoscope:* Westminster Records 8162.

Davis, Miles, from the album *Miles Davis and the Modern Jazz Giants:* Prestige Records 7650. From the album *Tallest Trees:* Prestige Records 24012.

Duchin, Eddy, from the album *The Eddy Duchin Story:* Columbia Records CS-9420.

Eldridge, Roy, from the album *Roy Eldridge:* Crescendo Records 9009.

Ferrante and Teicher, from the album *Greatest Love Themes of the Twentieth Century:* United Artist Records LA 101-G2.

Feyer, George, from the album *The Essential George Gershwin:* Vanguard Records VSD-61/62 and VSQ 40039/40.

Fitzgerald, Ella, from the album *Ella in London:* Pablo Records 2310711. From the album *Mack the Knife—Ella in Berlin:* Verve Records 6-4041.

Garner, Erroll from the album *Erroll Garner:* Savoy Records 12003.

Gillespie, Dizzy, from the album *Dizzy Gillespie.*

Gleason, Jackie, from the album *Tenderly:* Capitol Records STBB-510.

Gray, Wardell, from the album *Wardell Gray Memorial Album:* Prestige Records 7343.

Hampton, Lionel, and the All Stars, from the album *Star Dust:* MCA Records 198.

Heath, Ted, from the album *Palladium Performances:* London Records SP-44046.

Henke, Mel, from the album *Dig Mel Henke:* Contemporary Records 5001.

Holiday, Billie, from the album *Billie Holiday—Original Recordings:* Columbia Records C-32060. From the album *Billie Holiday Story—Volume 2:* Columbia KG-32124. From the album *Billie Holiday:* Columbia Records C3L-21.

Jackson, William, from the album *Soul Night—Live:* Prestige Records 7396.

James, Etta, from album *Funk:* Cadet Records 832.

Kostelanetz, Andre, from the album *Kostelanetz Plays Gershwin:* Columbia Records KG-32825.

Lee, Peggy, from the album *Folks Who Live on the Hill:* Capitol Records STBB-517.

McGhee, Howard, and Milt Jackson, from the album *Howard McGhee and Milt Jackson:* Savoy Records 12026.

Minnelli, Liza, from the album *Liza Minnelli, Four Sider:* A & M Records 3524. From the album *New Feelin':* A & M Records 4272.

Reinhardt, Django, and others, from the album *Parisian Swing:* Crescendo Records 9002.

Soundtrack/Diana Ross, from the album *Lady Sings the Blues:* Motown 758.

Stewart, Helyne, from the album *Love Moods:* Contemporary Records 7601.

Tatum, Art, from the album *Piano Starts Here:* Crescendo Records CS-9655. From the album *Art Tatum, Solo Masterpieces:* Pablo Records 2625703. From the album *Art Tatum:* Trip Records JT-9.

Vaughan, Sarah, from the album *Echoes of an Era:* Roulette Records RE-103.

Whiteman, Paul, from the album *The Twenties:* Columbia Records C3L-35.

William, Mary Lou, from the album *In London,* Crescendo Records 99029.

Young, Lester, and Coleman Hawkins, from the album *Classic Tenors:* Flying Dutchman 101146.

Fascinating Rhythm

Chacksfield, Frank, from the album *The Glory That Was Gershwin:* London Records SP-44194.

Feyer, George, from the album *The Essential George Gershwin:* Vanguard Records VSD-61/62 and VSQ 40039/40.

Grierson, Ralph, and Artie Kane, from the album *Gershwin 'S Wonderful:* Angel Records 36083.

Kessel, Barney from the album *Music to Listen To:* Contemporary Records 7521

Kostelanetz, Andre, from the album *Andre Kostelanetz Plays Gershwin:* Columbia Records KG-32825.

Light, Enoch, and the Light Brigade, from the album *Provocative Stereo Sounds of Our Time:* Command Records 981.

Merrill, Buddy, from the album *Guitar Sounds of Buddy Merrill:* Accent Records 5010. From the album *Best of Buddy Merrill:* Accent Records 5030.

Rodgers, Eric from the album *Percussive Twenties:* London Records SP-44006.

Maybe

Fitzgerald, Ella, from the album *Ella Sings Gershwin:* MCA Records 215.

Someone to Watch Over Me

Adler, Larry, from the album *Larry Adler Again:* Audio Fidelity Records 6193.

Austin, Claire, from the album *Claire Austin:* Contemporary Records 5002.

Austin, Sil, from the album *Sil and the Silver Screen:* SSS International Records 14.

Byrd, Donald, and others, from the album *Byrd's Word:* Savoy Records 12032.

Carter, Benny, from the album *Swingin' the Twenties:* Contemporary Records 7561.

Condon, Eddie, from the album *The Immortal Eddie Condon:* Olympic Records 7122.

Eldridge, Roy, from the album *Roy Eldridge:* Crescendo Records 9009.

Fitzgerald, Ella, from the album *Ella Sings Gershwin:* MCA Records 215.

Garner, Erroll, from the album *Magician:* London Records APS-640.

Gershwin, George, from the album *The Twenties:* Columbia Records C3L-35.

Grant, Earl, from the album *Just For a Thrill:* MCA Records 223.

Hawkins, Coleman, from the album *Capitol Jazz Classics—Volume 5:* Capitol Records M-11030.

Kesner, Dick, from the album *Intermezzo:* Brunswick Records 754054.

Kostelanetz, Andre, from the album *Sounds of Love:* Columbia Records GP-10. From the album *Andre Kostelanetz Plays Gershwin:* Columbia Records KG-32825.

Lawrence, Gertrude, from the album *The Star:* Audio Fidelity 709.

Light, Enoch, from the album *Best of Enoch Light:* Project 3 5027.

Merman, Ethel, from the album *Ethel's Ridin' High:* London Records XPS-909.

Paramor, Norrie, from the album *In London, In Love:* Capitol Records ST-10025.

Peterson, Oscar, from the album *Exclusively for My Friends:* MPS Records 25101.

Powell, Bud, from the album *Echoes of An Era:* Roulette Records RE-110.

Prysock, Arthur, from the album *Art and Soul:* Verve Records 6-5009.

Scott, Little Jimmy, from the album *The Soul of Little Jimmy Scott:* Savoy Records 12300.

Shearing, George, from the album *Early Years:* Everest Records 236.

Sinatra, Frank, from the album *My One and Only Love:* Capitol Records STBB-724.

Streisand, Barbra, from the album *My Name Is Barbra:* Columbia Records CS-9136.

Tatum, Art, from the album *Capitol Jazz Classics—Volume 8:* Capitol Records M-11028. From the album *Piano Starts Here:* Columbia Records CS-9655. From the album *Art Tatum, Solo Masterpieces:* Pablo Records 2625703. From the album *The Essential Art Tatum:* Verve Records 6-8433.

Webster, Ben, from the album *See You at the Fair:* Impulse Records 65.

'S Wonderful

Charleston City All Stars, from the album *Roaring 20's:* Westminster Records GAS-68004.

Conniff, Ray, from the album *Ray Conniff's Greatest Hits:* Columbia Records CS-9839.

Haig, Al, from the album *Al Haig Trio and Quintet:* Prestige Records 7841.

Heath, Ted, from the album *All Time Top Twelve:* London Records PS-117.

Kostelanetz, Andre, from the album *Andre Kostelanetz Plays Gershwin:* Columbia Records KG-32825.

Lombardo, Guy, from the album *Guy Lombardo:* Capitol Records STCL-578.

Shaw, Artie, from the album *This Is Artie Shaw—Volume 2:* Victor Records VPM 6062.

Smith, Paul, from the album *By the Fireside:* Savoy Records 12094.

Stitt, Sonny, from the album *Stitt's Bits:* Prestige Records 7585. From the album *Genesis:* Prestige Records 24044.

Van Damme, Art, from the album *Star Spangled Rhythm:* MPS Records MC-25157.

Embraceable You

Aldrich, Ronnie, from the album *Romantic Pianos of Ronnie Aldrich:* London Records SP-44042.

Anthony, Ray, from the album *Ray Anthony Plays for Dream:* Capitol Records ST-723.

Bechet, Sidney, from the album *Sidney Bechet:* Crescendo Records 99012.

Boston Pops Orchestra, with Arthur Fiedler, from the album *Greatest Hits of the 30's:* Victor Records ARLI-0042. From the album (with Peter Nero) *Fiedler and His Friends:* Victor Records LSC-3199. From the album (with Peter Nero) *Greatest Hit Songs:* Victor Records ARLI-0510.

Chacksfield, Frank, from the album *The Glory That Was Gershwin:* London Records SP-44194.

Charles, Ray, from the album *Moods of Love:* ABC Records X-772.

Clark, Kenny, from the album *Paris de Bop Sessions:* Prestige Records 7605.

Coleman, Ornette, from the album *This Is Our Magic:* Atlantic Recording Corp. 1353. From the album *Best of Ornette Coleman:* Atlantic Recording Corp. 1558.

Condon, Eddie, from the album (with Bud Freeman) *Commodore Years:* Atlantic Recording Corp. 2-309.

Davis, Miles, from the album *Miles Davis:* Everest Records 283. From the album *Miles of Jazz:* Trip Records 5015.

Davison, Wild Bill, from the album *Wild Bill Davison Plays the Greatest . . . :* Dixieland Jubilee Records 508.

Evans, Bill, Trio, from the album *The Bill Evans Trio:* Verve Records 6-8762.

Garland, Judy, from the album *Judy Garland Collector's Items:* MCA Records 2-4046.

Hackett, Bobby, and others, from the album *Strike Up the Band:* Flying Dutchman BDLI.0829.

Hawes, Hampton, from the album *Everybody Likes Hampton Hawes:* Contemporary Records 3523.

Hawkins, Eldridge-Brown-Jones, All Stars, from the album *The Newport Years—Volume 4:* Verve Records 6-8829. From the album *Giants of the Tenor Saxophone:* Columbia Records KG-32774.

Holiday, Billie, from the album *Strange Fruit:* Atlantic Recording Corp. 1614.

Johnson, J.J., and others, from the album *The Birdlanders:* Everest Records 275.

Jordan, Duke, from the album *Jorud:* Prestige Records 7849. From the album *Jazz Laboratory:* Savoy Records 12145.

Kesner, Dick, from the album *Dick Kesner/Magic Stradivarius:* Brunswick Records 754051.

Kessel, Barney, from the album *Barney Kessel:* Contemporary Records 3513.

Kloss, Eric, from the album *Introducing Eric Kloss:* Prestige Records 7442.

Mantovani, from the album *Mantovani . . . Memories:* London Records PS-542.

McGriff, Jimmy, from the album *I've Got A New Woman:* Solid State Records 18030.

McPherson, Jones, and Harris, from the album *Bebop Revisited:* Prestige Records 7359.

Mingus, Charles, from the album *My Favorite Quintet:* Fantasy Records JWS-5.

Nero, Peter, with the Boston Pops Orchestra, from the album *Love Is a Music for Every Mood:* Victor Records: LSC-3223.

O'Connell, Helen, from the album *This Is Helen O'Connell:* Victor Records VPM-6076.

Paramor, Norrie, from the album *In London, In Love:* Capitol Records ST-10025.

Parker, Charlie from the album *Charlie Parker:* Prestige Records 24009.

Powell, Bud, from the album *Broadcast Performance:* ESP-Disc Records BUD-1. From the album *Bud Powell Trio:* Fantasy Records 86006. From the album (with others) *Greatest Jazz Concert Ever:* Prestige Records 24024.

Sinatra, Frank, from the album *Frank Sinatra Deluxe Set:* Capitol Records STFL-2841.

Supersax, from the album *Salt Peanuts:* Capitol Records ST-11271.

Tatum, Art, from the album *Art Tatum, Solo Masterpieces:* Pablo Records 2625703.

Williams, Andy, from the album *Warm and Willing:* Columbia Records CS-8679. From the album *Sound of Music/Andy Williams:* Columbia Records KGP-5.

Witherspoon, Jimmy, from the album *Blues for Easy Livers:* Prestige Records 7475.

Bidin' My Time

Boston Pops Orchestra, with Peter Nero, from the album *Greatest Hits of the 30's—Volume 2:* Victor Records ARLI-0506.

Pink Floyd, from the album *Relics:* Harvest Records SW-759.

I Got Rhythm

Bechet, S., and Lionel Hampton, from the album *Sidney Bechet:* Everest Records 228.

Chacksfield, Frank, from the album *The Glory That Was Gershwin:* London Records SP-44194.

Christian, Charles, from the album *Solo Flight:* Columbia Records G-30779.

Condon, Eddie from the album *Eddie Condon's World of Jazz:* Columbia Records KG-31564. From the album (with Bud Freeman) *Commodore Years:* Atlantic Recording Corp. 2-309.

Faith, Percy, from the album *Chinatown:* Columbia Records KC & CQ 33244.

Ferrante and Teicher, from the album *Nostalgic Hits:* ABC Records X-791.

Garland, Judy, from the album *Judy Garland Collector's Item:* MCA Records 2-4046.

Goodman, Benny, from the album *All-Time Greatest Hits:* Columbia Records KG-31547. From the album (with Quartet) *Carnegie Hall Jazz Concert:* Columbia Records OSL-160. From the album *From Spirituals to Swing:* Vanguard Records VSD-47/48.

Hawes, Hampton, from the album *Hampton Hawes Trio:* Contemporary Records 33505.

Krupa, Gene, from the album *The Best of Verve's Choice:* Verve Records 6-8594.

Light, Enoch, and Light Brigade, from the album *Torchy Thirties:* Westminster Records WGAS-68012.

Merman, Ethel, from the album *Merman Sings Merman:* London Records XPS-901.

Miller, Glenn, from the album *Big Bands' Greatest Hits:* Columbia Records G-30009.

Nero, Peter, from the album (with Boston Pops) *Nero Goes "Pops":* Victor Records LSC-2821.

Patto, from the album *Roll 'em, Smoke 'em Put Another Line Out:* Island Records SW-9322.

Redman, Don, from the album *World of Swing:* Columbia Records KG-32945.

Reinhardt, Django, from the album *Django '35-'39:* Crescendo Records 39019.

Streisand, Barbra, from the album *Barbra Streisand and Other Musical Hits:* Columbia Records KC-32655.

Sutton, Ralph, from the album *Knocked Out Nocturne:* Project 3 5040.

Tatum, Art, from the album *Art Tatum Masterpieces:* MCA Records 2-4019.

Waller, Fats, from the album *Valentine Stomp:* Victor Records LPV-525.

Wells, Dicky, from the album *Dicky Wells in Paris, 1937:* Prestige Records 7593.

Whiteman, Paul, from the album *Paul Whiteman's Cavalcade of Music:* Westminster Records WGAS-68013.

Williams, Roger, from the album *Roger Williams Greatest Hits:* MCA Records 63.

Wilson, Teddy, Trio, from the album *The Newport Years—Volume 2:* Verve Records 6-8827. From the album *Teddy Wilson:* Crescendo Records 9014.

Young, Lester, and Coleman Hawkins, from the album *Classic Tenors:* Flying Dutchman 310146.

Strike Up the Band

Bechet, Sidney, from the album *Sidney Bechet:* Crescendo Records 9012.

Bennett, Tony, and Count Basie, from the album *Echoes of an Era—Basie Vocal Years:* Roulette Records RE-107.

Boston Pops Orchestra, with Arthur Fiedler, from the album *Yankee Doodle Dandy:* Victor Records LSC-3200. From the album *Greatest Hits of the 20's:* Victor Records ARLI-0041.

Brown, Odell, from the album *Raisin the Roof:* Cadet Records 775.

Chacksfield, Frank, from the album *The Glory That Was Gershwin:* London Records SP-44194.

Grierson, Ralph, and Artie Kane, from the album *Gershwin's—'S Wonderful:* Angel Records 36083.

Hackett, Buddy, and others, from the album *Strike Up the Band:* Flying Dutchman BDLI-0829.

Heath, Ted, from the album *Ted Heath [Big Band]:* Everest Records 251.

Jordan, Duke, from the album *Jordu:* Prestige Records 7849.

Kostelanetz, Andre, from the album *That's Entertainment:* Columbia Records KG-33065. From the album *Andre Kostelanetz Plays Gershwin:* Columbia Records KG-32825. From the album *Stereo Wonderland of Sound-Star:* Columbia Records CS-8518.

Mann, Herbie, from the album *Et Tu Flute:* Verve Records 2V6-8821.

McPartland, Marian, from the album *Marian McPartland:* Savoy Records 12004. From the album *Great Britain:* Savoy Records 12016.

Peabody, Eddie, from the album *16 Great Performances:* ABC Records DP-4010.

Stitt, Sonny, from the album *Soul Electricity:* Prestige Records 7635. From the album *Bud's Blues:'* Prestige Records 7839. From the album *Genesis:* Prestige Records 24044.

Tijuana Brass, from the album *Summertime:* A & M Records 4314.

I've Got A Crush on You

Ferrante and Teicher, from the album *Ferrante and Teicher, Love Themes:* United Artists Records 6282.

Fitzgerald, Ella, from the album *Ella Fitzgerald—Newport Jazz Festival:* Columbia Records KG-32557. From the album *Ella Sings Gershwin:* MCA Records 215. From the album *Newport Years—Volume I:* Verve Records 6-8826.

Freeman, Stan, from the album *Fascination:* Project 3 5012.

Hackett, Bobby, from the album *What a Wonderful World:* Flying Dutchman 10159.

Keating, Johnny, from the album *Swing Revisited:* London Records SP-44034.

Sinatra, Frank, from the album *Nice 'N' Easy:* Capitol Records SM-1417. From the album *Round No. 1:* Capitol Records SABB-11357. From the album *In the Beginning:* Columbia Records KG-31358. From the album (with Count Basie) *Sinatra at the Sands* (in concert): Reprise Records 2-1019.

Tatum, Art, from the album *Art Tatum, Solo Masterpieces:* Pablo Records 2625703.

Of Thee I Sing

O'Connor, Carroll, and Cloris Leachman, and others, from the TV Soundtrack album *Of Thee I Sing:* Columbia Records S-31763.

Love Is Sweeping the Country

O' Connor, Carroll, Cloris Leachman, and others, from a special TV broadcast, from the album *Of Thee I Sing:* Columbia Records S-31763.

Fisher, Eddie, Frankie Carle, Eartha Kitt, Jayne P. Morgan, and others, from the album *The Popular Gershwin:* RCA Victor LPM-6000.

Let's Call the Whole Thing Off

Cooke, Sam, from the album *Collection of Memories:* Trip Records X-9517.

Fitzgerald, Ella, and Louis Armstrong, from the album *Ella and Louis:* Verve Records 6-8811.

Holiday, Billie, from the album *Billie Holiday Golden Years—Volume 2:* Columbia Records SC3L-40. From the album *Billie Holiday Story Volume 2:* Columbia Records KG-32124.

Nice Work If You Can Get It

Allen, Henry, from the album *Henry Allen "Red", Memorial Album:* Prestige Records 7755.

Astaire, Fred, from the album *Nothing Thrilled Us Half As Much:* Epic Records 15103.

Fitzgerald, Ella, from the album *Ella Fitzgerald—Newport Jazz Festival:* Columbia Records KG-32557. From the album *Ella Sings Gershwin:* MCA Records 215.

Gillespie, Dizzy, from the album *In the Beginning:* Prestige Records 24030.

Goodman, Benny, Trio, from the album *King of Swing:* Columbia Records OSL-180.

Hines, Earl, from the album *Earl Hines "Fatha":* Everest Records 246.

Holiday, Billie, from the album *Billie Holiday Golden Years—Volume 2:* Columbia Records C3L-40. From the album *Billie Holiday Story—Volume 3:* Columbia Records KG-32127. From the album *Newport Years—Volume 1:* Verve Records 6-8826.

Mehegan, H. John, from the album *Reflections:* Savoy Records 12028.

Niehaus, Lennie, from the album *Lennie Niehaus:* Contemporary Records 5503.

Sinatra, Frank, and Count Basie, from the album *Sinatra—Basie:* Reprise Records 1008. From the album *My Kind of Broadway:* Reprise Records 1015.

Staton, Dakota, from the album *Dakota '67:* London Records PS-495.

Stitt, Sonny, from the album *Stitt's Bits:* Prestige Records 7585. From the album *Genesis:* Prestige Records 2044.

Tatum, Art, from the album *Capitol Jazz Classics—Volume 3:* Capitol Records M-11028.

A Foggy Day

Astaire, Fred, from the album *Nothing Thrilled Us Half As Much:* Epic Records 15103.

Byrd, Charlie, from the album *Jazz Recital:* Savoy Records 12099.

Chacksfield, Frank, from the album *Globetrotting:* London Records SP-44059.

Dee, Lenny, from the album *Lenny Dee Tour:* MCA Records 234. From the album *Best of Lenny Dee:* MCA Records 2-4042.

Ferrante and Teicher, from the album *Ferrante and Teicher:* United Artist Records UXS-77.

Fitzgerald, Ella, and Louis Armstrong, from the album *Ella and Louis:* Verve Records 6-8811. From the album (with J. Pass) *Take Love Easy:* Pablo Records 2310702.

Garland, Judy, from the album *Judy at Carnegie Hall:* Capitol Records SWBO-1569.

Jamal, Ahmad, from the album *Chamber Music of the New Jazz:* Cadet Records 602.

Kostelanetz, Andre, from the album *Andre Kostelanetz Plays Gershwin:* Columbia Records KG-32825.

Lombardo, Guy, from the album *Dance Medley Time:* MCA Records 242.

McLean, Jackie, from the album *Lights Out:* Prestige Records 7757.

McRae, Carmen, from the album *Carmen McRae In Person:* Mainstream Records 352.

Mingus, Charles, from the album *The Art of Charles Mingus:* Atlantic Recording Corp. 2-302. From the album *Charles Mingus, Quin, plus Max Roach:* Fantasy Records 86009. From the album *Charles Mingus:* Prestige Records 24010.

Moore, Oscar, from the album *Great Guitars of Jazz:* MGM Records 4691.

Muller, Werner, from the album *On the Move:* London Records SP-44026.

Quadrastrings, from the album *Hollywood Gold—Volume 1:* Ovation Records QD-1601.

Sinatra, Frank, from the album *My One and Only Love:* Capitol Records STBB-724. From the album *Ring-A-Ding Ding:* Reprise Records 1001.

Smith, Johnny, and Stan Getz, from the album *Echoes of an Era—Smith-Getz Years:* Roulette Records RE-106.

Staton, Dakota, from the album *Late Late Show:* Capitol Records SM-876.

Stewart, Billy, from the album *Unbelievable:* Chess Records 1499.

Van Damme, Art, and others, from the album *Squeezing Art and Tender Flutes:* MPS Records MB-21755.

Vaughan, Sarah, from the album *Sarah Vaughan "Live" in Japan:* Mainstream Records 2-401.

Preludes 1-3

Heifetz, Jascha, from the album *Heifetz Plays Gershwin:* Victor Records LSC-2856.

Jamanis, Michael, from the album *Piano Music of Gershwin:* Connoisseur Society Q-2067.

Levant, Oscar, from the album *Gershwin's Greatest Hits:* Columbia Records MS-7518.

List, Eugene, from the album *Rhapsody in Blue:* Turnabout Records 34457.

Pennario, Leonard, from the album *Gershwin's Greatest Hits:* Victor Records LSC-5001.

Rhapsody in Blue

Bernstein, Leonard, and Columbia Symphony Orchestra, from the album *Gershwin's Greatest Hits:* Columbia Records MS-7518.

Black, Stanley, and London Symphony Orchestra, from the album *Rhapsody in Blue:* London Records SPC-21009.

Boston Pops, with Arthur Fiedler, from the album *Greatest Hits of the 20's:* Victor Records ARLI-0041.

Byrne, Bobby, from the album *Great Song Hits of the Glen Miller Orchestra:* Westminster Records WGAS-680011.

Chacksfield, Frank, from the album *The Glory That Was Gershwin:* London Records SP-44194.

Dee, Lenny, from the album *Lenny Dee:* MCA Records 379.

Deodata, from the album *Deodata:* CTI Records Q-6029.

Entremont, Philippe, and the Philadelphia Orchestra, from the album *Gershwin Album:* Columbia Records MG-30073.

Feyer, George, from the album *Essential George Gershwin:* Vanguard Records VSQ-40039/40.

Gershwin, George, from the album *George Gershwin In Concert:* Everest Records 914. From the album *Gershwin Plays Gershwin:* Everest Records 3371.

Haas, Werner, and Monte Carlo Opera, from the album *Rhapsody in Blue:* Philips Records 6500118.

Kostelanetz, Andre, from the album *That's Entertainment:* Columbia Records KG-33065. From the album (with Andre Previn) *Concerto in F:* Columbia Records CS-8286. From the album (with Andre Previn) *Andre Kostelanetz Plays Gershwin:* Columbia Records KG-32825.

Levant, Oscar, and Philadelphia Orchestra, from the album *Piano Music of Gershwin:* Columbia Records CS-8641.

List, Eugene, and the Berlin Symphony Orchestra, from the album *Rhapsody in Blue:* Turnabout Records 34457.

London Symphony Orchestra, from the album *250 Years of Film Music:* Columbia Records CS-32381.

Lowenthal, Jerome, and the Utah Symphony Orchestra, from the album *Rhapsody in Blue:* Vanguard Records 10017.

Nero, Peter, and Boston Pops Orchestra, from the album *Gershwin's* Victor Records LSC-5001.

Nero, Peter, and Andre Kostelanetz, from the album *Quadraphonic Concert:* Columbia Records CQ-32147.

Nero, Peter, and the Boston Pops Orchestra, from the album *Gershwin's Greatest Hits:* Victor Records LSC-5001.

Nibley, Reid, and Utah Symphony Orchestra, from the album *Rhapsody in Blue:* Westminster Records WGS-8122.

Pennario, Leonard, and Hollywood Bowl Symphony, from the album *Rhapsody in Blue:* Seraphim Records 60174.

Previn, Andre, and the London Symphony Orchestra, from the album *Rhapsody in Blue:* Angel Records 36810. From the album (with the Columbia Symphony Orchestra) *Great Moments from the Promenades:* Columbia Records MG 31415.

Sanroma, Jesus, and the Pittsburgh Symphony Orchestra, from the album *Rhapsody in Blue:* Everest Records 3067.

Veri, Earl and Boston Pops Orchestra, from the album *Rhapsody in Blue:* Victor Records LSC-2367. From the album *Rhapsody in Blue:* Victor Records LSC-2746.

Veri, Frances, and Michael Jamanis, from the album *Rhapsody in Blue:* Connoisseur Society Q-2054.

Victorian Trumpet Trio, from the album *Australia's Fabulous Trumpets:* Key Records 591.

Wild, Earl, and the Boston Pops Orchestra from the album *Rhapsody in Blue:* Victor Records LSC-2367. From the album *Rhapsody in Blue:* Victor Records LSC-2746.